Variety With Venison
and
Other Wild Game

Recipes by: Delores Green and Connie White

Marinating and Preparation by Connie White

Cover and Illustrations by Terry Groner

Variety With Venison
and
Other Wild Game

Published by:

Green & White Publishing Co.
2108 Spring Arbor Rd.
Jackson, MI 49203

Recipes

Equivalent & Substitution Chart

SUBSTITUTIONS

Ingredient	Amount	Substitution
Rice (3-4 c. cooked)	1 c. regular, uncooked	1 c. converted, uncooked 1 c. brown, uncooked 1 c. wild rice, uncooked 2 c. precooked
Tomato juice	1 cup	1/2 c. tomato sauce with 1/2 c. water

	Equivalent Measures	Equivalent Measures
Dash or pinch	= Less than 1/8 teaspoon	= 2 to 3 drops
1 tablespoon	= 3 teaspoons	= 1/2 fluid ounce
1/4 cup	= 4 tablespoons	= 2 fluid ounces
1/3 cup	= 5 tablespoons + 1 teas.	= 2.5 fluid ounces
1/2 cup	= 8 tablespoons	= 4 fluid ounces
3/4 cup	= 12 tablespoons	= 6 fluid ounces
1 cup	= 16 tablespoons	= 8 fluid ounces
1 pint	= 2 cups	= 16 fluid ounces
1 quart	= 2 pints	= 32 fluid ounces
1 gallon	= 4 quarts	= 32 fluid ounces
1 pound	= 2 cups	= 16 ounces

SECTION ONE

VENISON RECIPES

TABLE OF CONTENTS

Venison Marinating and Preparation Suggestions

To begin, we would like to give the definition of venison, that being: the flesh of a game animal, especially the deer, used as food. Also be aware that a deer is any hoofed, cud-chewing animal, the male of which bears antlers that are shed annually. The meat used in the recipes of this book could be from any animal of the deer family such as a doe, a buck, the antelope or the elk.

Most wild game such as deer, usually feed on items like field corn, fruits, sweet grass (mostly out west) and nuts. You will find that acorns and beech nuts are main crops for deer, although the Eastern White Tail Deer feed off the tender buds of new trees. Antelope feed mostly on sage brush. You will also find that the most tender of meats come from the young deer.

However, in the following paragraphs we will attempt to offer some tips on how to marinate and prepare your venison to offer the most tender recipes possible.

First we'll make note that some deer have a strong gamey flavor to them. The easiest way to modify the flavor is to soak the meat in a bowl of vinegar and water(about 1/3 vinegar to 2/3 water) for about 2 hours. Note here that red vinegar is stronger while white vinegar is more delicate. After soaking meat in vinegar, dry thoroughly with a paper towel to eliminate any vinegar taste.

Another method is to scald the meat by pouring boiling water over it and then draining.

Vinegar is also a good tenderizer. A touch of olive oil is also good for tenderizing. Milk is good for tenderizing the liver. Just refrigerate for about 2 hours, remove and then dry thoroughly. Also note that venison liver should be cleaned thoroughly and sliced thinly before freezing.

It is always best to soak meat 8 to 24 hours before cooking, turning from time to time. You will find though, that meat tenderizes more rapidly at room temperature rather than under refrigeration.

One last note we would like to offer and that is the neck meat and the shanks can be separated and cut into 1 to 2 inch strips for sirloin tips. Also note that on any recipe using ground venison, 1 tablespoon of beef bouillon may be added per pound to modify the flavor.

We hope you will enjoy all of our recipes as much as we have enjoyed preparing them for you.

Meatballs & Snacks

Apricot Venison Meatballs for Fondue

1 lb. ground venison
2 tsp. beef broth granules
1/2 cup dry bread crumbs
1 egg
1 c. chopped dried apricots
pepper to taste

Combine all ingredients in bowl and mix thoroughly. Shape into small meatballs for fondue.

Sweet Venison Meatballs

3 - 12oz. jars of chili sauce, brand of choice
1 - 12oz. jar of grape jelly, brand of choice
2 lbs. ground venison

Cook chili sauce and jelly in medium sauce pan until well blended. Form venison meatballs. Add to sauce and simmer on low heat about one hour.

Venison Salami

2 lbs. ground venison
2 tsp. curing salt
3/4 tsp. garlic salt
1 tsp. mustard seed
1/4 tsp. black pepper
1/4 tsp. red pepper
1 c. water

Combine all ingredients and mix well. Divide into 3 parts and form into long rolls. Wrap each roll in heavy foil. Refrigerate 24 hours. Place wrapped rolls in large pan and cover with cold water. Bring to boil and boil 1 hour. Remove salami from foil and drain on cooling rack. Chill before slicing. Meat may be pinkish, but will be fully cooked.

Venison & Sausage Meatballs

1/2 lb. ground venison
1/2 lb. sausage
1 1/2 cups bisquick mix
1 c. grated cheese

Thoroughly mix together all ingredients. Form into 1" meatballs. Bake in oven 400 degrees for 20 to 30 minutes turning once.

Yields 2 to 2 1/2 dozen meatballs.

Venison Meatballs and Sauce

Meatballs

1 1/2 lbs. ground venison
3/4 c. oats, uncooked
1/3 c. chopped onion
1 tsp. salt
1/4 tsp. oregano
1/4 tsp. pepper
1 egg
1/2 c. milk

Sauce

1/3 c. chopped onion
1/3 c. chopped green pepper
1 - 16oz. can tomatoes
1 - 8oz. can tomato sauce
1/2 tsp. salt
1/8 tsp. garlic powder
1/4 tsp. cayenne
1/4 tsp. oregano
1 bay leaf
1/2 lb. ground venison

For meatballs, combine all ingredients. Shape to form meatballs. Brown in small amount of shortening in large skillet. Remove meatballs.

For sauce, in same skillet, lightly brown onion and green pepper in drippings. Add remaining
ingredients. Simmer over low heat about 20 minutes. Add meatballs to sauce; cover and simmer another 40 minutes. Remove bay leaf before serving.

Yields 6 servings.

Swedish Venison Meatballs

1 lb. ground venison
1/4 lb. ground pork
1/2 c. minced onion
1/2 to 3/4 c. bread crumbs
1 tsp. worcestershire sauce
1 egg
1/2 c. flour

2 tsp. beef broth granules
1/2 tsp. black pepper
1/2 tsp. salt
1 c. sour cream
1/4 c. oil
3/4 tsp. paprika

Combine venison, pork, onion, bread crumbs, worcestershire sauce, egg, beef broth granules and black pepper in a large bowl; mix well and shape into small meatballs. Brown in skillet; remove from skillet and set aside. Combine flour, paprika and salt. Stir into pan drippings. Add approximately 2 1/4 cups of water stirring constantly. Return meatballs to gravy. Cook for 20 minutes or until tender. Remove from heat and blend in sour cream.

NOTE: These meatballs may be used for fondue. If so, add 1 teaspoon of flour to mixture.

Venison Meatball Kabobs

1 1/2 lbs. ground venison
1 c. oatmeal
1/2 tsp. pepper
1/2 c. tomato sauce
1/2 tsp. extra spicy Mrs. Dash
8 small whole cooked potatoes
2 med. green peppers or 1 red & 1 green (cut into 8 pieces)
4 med. tomatoes (cut into 8 pieces)

1 T. beef bouillon granules
1 egg beaten
1 T. worcestershire sauce
1/2 c. bread crumbs
24 med. stuffed olives
8 large fresh whole mushrooms
1 c. barbecue sauce

Combine first 9 ingredients. Mix well. Shape meat mixture around stuffed olives. Alternate 3 meatballs, 2 tomato wedges, 2 pepper strips, 1 potato and 1 mushroom on 8 skewers. Brush with barbecue sauce. Place kabobs over coals about 6 to 7 inches from source of heat. Cook 7 to 8 minutes each side. Add more barbecue sauce and cook 3 minutes longer on each side. Longer for well done.

Yields 8 servings.

Venison Porcupine Balls

1 1/2 lbs. ground venison
1/2 c. uncooked rice
1 tsp. salt
1/2 tsp. pepper
2 celery stalks
2 med. onions
2 qts. tomato juice

Wash rice and mix with ground venison, salt and pepper. Form into one inch balls. Pack loose in pressure cooker. Dice celery and onion. Place in cooker. Cover with tomato juice. Cook on ten pound pressure for 10 minutes.

Balls may be browned in frying pan, then placed in deep roaster and simmered for 30 minutes.

Venison Jerky

3 lbs. venison
2 tsp. salt
5 T. sugar
1/8 tsp. cinnamon
1/4 tsp. 5 spice powder
2 T. soy sauce
2 T. red cooking wine
1 tsp. msg

Partially freeze meat; cut along grain into 3 inch strips. Mix all remaining ingredients together. Marinate meat in mixture 24 hours in deep bowl. Bake at 350 degrees until brown; approximately 15 minutes. Turn only once.

Venison Crescent Snack

1 8oz. can refrigerated crescent
dinner rolls
1 1/2 c. cooked venison, diced or 1/2
lb. ground venison
2 T. butter or margarine
1 1/4 tsp. mustard
1/4 c. finely chopped green onion
1/4 c. finely chopped green pepper
1 1/2 c. shredded mozzarella or
cheddar cheese

Unroll dough. Press into 13x9 inch
pan; seal seams. Combine margarine
and mustard; spread over dough.
Sprinkle venison, onion and green
pepper over crust. Top with cheese.
Bake at 375 degrees for 20 minutes.
Cut and serve.

Yields 24 snacks.

Hot Venison Dip

1 lb. ground venison
1 tsp. beef bouillon granules
16 oz. Velveeta cheese
1 can Hormel chili with beans

Mix bouillon granules with venison.
Brown in skillet until done. Melt
Velveeta cheese. Add chili and
venison. Serve hot with corn chips.

Steaks & Chops

Baked Onion Smothered Venison Steak

6 - 8oz. venison steaks
1 large onion, finely chopped
1 pkg. dry onion soup mix
1/2 tsp. pepper
2 tsp. soy sauce
2 tsp. worcestershire sauce
1 tsp. beef broth granules

Marinate steaks for about 2 hours with 1 tsp. soy sauce & 1 tsp. worcestershire sauce. Add pepper and coat with flour. Place in skillet with small amount of shortening. Brown steaks; place in baking dish. Mix onion soup with 2 cups of water. Add chopped onions, 1 tsp. soy sauce & 1 tsp. worcestershire sauce to soup. Pour over steaks. Simmer for 1 hour or until tender. Yields 6 servings.

Cantonese Sauce Venison Fry

2 T. soy sauce
1 T. teriyaki sauce
1 T. chopped onion
1/4 c. chopped green pepper
2 T. cooking oil
1/2 c. prepared sweet/sour sauce
2 T. garlic flakes
2 T. apple cider vinegar
6 - 8oz. venison steaks

Soak venison steaks in boiled hot water until water cools; drain & dry. Mix next 6 ingredients together in small pan. Saute until peppers & onions are tender. Sprinkle apple cider vinegar on dry steaks. Place in skillet. Add garlic flakes. Cook on low heat until brown. Pour sauce over steaks & continue cooking until done. Turn occasionally.

Chili Bean Venison Steak

6 to 8 - 8oz. venison steaks
seasoned meat tenderizer
1/4 c. chopped onions
1/4 tsp. instant minced garlic
2 T. apple cider vinegar
2 T. worcestershire sauce
3 T. cooking oil or butter

3 tsp. chili powder
1 - 8oz. can tomato sauce
juice of 1 lemon slice
2 T. brown sugar
1 1/2 tsp. prepared mustard
1/4 tsp. tabasco sauce
1 -16oz. can chili beans

Soak steaks in boiled hot water until water cools; remove and dry. Sprinkle meat with tenderizer. Let stand for 15 minutes. Combine onion, garlic, vinegar, cooking oil, worcestershire sauce and chili powder to make marinade. Pour over steak. Let stand 20 minutes. Remove steak from marinade. Combine marinade with remaining ingredients, except beans, in sauce pan. Simmer for 12 minutes. Place steak in shallow baking dish; spoon sauce over steak. Bake in 325 degree oven for 1 hour. Add beans. Bake 20 minutes longer.

Yields 6 to 8 servings.

Venison Mushroom Steak

6 - 8oz. venison steaks
1 c. vinegar
2 - 4oz. cans mushrooms
steak tenderizer
salt & pepper
1 T. garlic flakes
2 T. soy sauce
2 T. A-1 sauce
2 T. worcestershire sauce
4 T. butter or margarine
juice of 1 lemon

Soak steaks in vinegar water for 1 hour; rinse & dry. Marinate with soy sauce & steak sauces for 1 hour. Add meat tenderizer; let stand for 1 hour. Add salt & pepper. Mix lemon juice with garlic flakes. Add to steak & cook in skillet with butter until brown. Add mushrooms & cook until tender.

Venison Salisbury Steak

1 lb. ground venison
1 tsp. beef broth granules
1/4 c. evaporated milk
1/2 tsp. black pepper
1/2 tsp. worcestershire sauce
4 tsp. barbecue sauce
1 c. crushed corn flakes/crackers
1 T. parmesan cheese
2 T. bacon drippings
2 T. flour
1 can beef broth bouillon

Mix first 8 ingredients together and form into patties. Brown in bacon drippings. Remove from skillet. Add flour to drippings in skillet, stirring constantly until smooth. Add beef broth & bring to a boil. Place patties back into skillet. Simmer over low heat until done. Serve with rice or potatoes. Add mushrooms if desired.

German Venison Steak

8 med. sized venison steaks
1 - 14oz. bottle catsup
14oz. water
1/4 c. sugar
1 medium chopped onion
2 T. beef broth granules
1/2 tsp. salt; pepper to taste
3 eggs
2 c. cracker crumbs
1/4 c. onion flakes

Soak steaks in 1 cup vinegar with water for 2 hours; rinse & dry. Combine catsup, water, onion, sugar & pepper in sauce pan. Simmer for 15 minutes. Combine beef broth granules, cracker crumbs & onion flakes. Beat eggs. Dip steaks in eggs. Roll in cracker crumb mixture. Place in skillet & brown on both sides. Remove to baking dish. Cover with sauce & bake at 300 degrees for one and a half hours.

Mandarin Orange Venison Chops

6 venison chops, 3/4" thick
2 T. oil
1/4 c. light karo syrup
1 c. mandarin orange slices
2 c. warm water
1/2 c. flour
1/2 tsp. salt
1/2 tsp. black pepper
1/4 tsp. thyme

Heat orange slices & water in medium sauce pan. Drain. In small mixing bowl combine flour, salt, pepper & thyme. Dust over both sides of chops. Heat oil in large frying pan. Brown chops in oil on both sides. Combine orange slices & karo syrup and pour over chops. Cover & cook 1 hour over low heat until chops are tender.
Yields 6 servings.

Mushroom Venison With Cheese

6 to 8 med. sized venison steaks
seasoned meat tenderizer
dash of tabasco sauce
1/2 c. soy sauce
2 tsp. instant minced onion
2 bay leaves, crushed

1/4 c. water
1 - 10 1/2 oz. cream of mushroom-soup
1/2 c. grated cheddar cheese
1 tsp. worcestershire sauce
1 - 4oz. can sliced mushrooms

Soak steaks in vinegar water for 1 hour; rinse and dry meat. Add meat tenderizer; let stand while mixing next 4 ingredients together. Place steaks in large skillet and pour mixture over steaks and brown on both sides. Reduce heat; add water and simmer covered for 20 to 30 minutes turning meat occasionally. Add remaining ingredients. Continue to simmer, stirring occasionally for another 10 to 15 minutes until cheese is melted and meat is tender.

Yields 6 to 8 servings.

Venison Chop Bake

6 venison chops, 3/4" thick
5 med. pared & thinly sliced potatoes
1 - 4oz. can sliced mushrooms
2 T. beef broth granules
1 c. water

1 envelope onion soup mix
1 c. vinegar
1 T. worcestershire sauce
1 T. soy sauce
pepper

Soak chops for 1 hour in 1 cup vinegar and enough water to cover chops. Rinse and dry thoroughly. Mix beef broth granules, soy sauce and worcestershire sauce. Brush on chops, both sides, and let stand for 1 hour. Preheat oven to 350 degrees. In large skillet, place chops; add pepper and fry until brown. Drain chops on paper towel. Butter bottom and sides of a 2 quart dish and place layers of potatoes and mushrooms. Top with chops. In small bowl mix onion soup with water. Pour over meat. Cover baking dish with foil and bake 1 1/2 hours or until potatoes are tender.

Yields 6 servings.

Cajun Venison Steak

6 -8 venison steaks
extra spicy Mrs. Dash
1 c. flour
4 T. oil

Spinkle extra spicy Mrs. Dash on both sides of steaks. Roll in flour. Heat oil in skillet to 350 degrees. Fry steaks until golden brown, turning only once.

Venison Steak & Gravy

6 venison steaks
1 can cream mushroom soup
2 beef bouillon cubes
salt & pepper to taste
2 T. oil
2 c. boiling water

Soak steak one hour in vinegar and water solution. Drain; cover with water, add 1 tsp. salt and soak one more hour. Wash; dry steaks with paper towel. Spinkle each side of steaks with salt, pepper and nutmeg. Roll in flour. Fry steaks in hot oil just until brown. Place steaks in baking dish. Add bouillon cubes to water, mix with soup. Pour over steaks. Bake at 300 degrees for 2 hours.

Yields 6 servings.

Tasty Venison Steak Bake

4 - 6 venison steaks
1 med. onion, sliced
1/2 c. butter or margarine
1 can tomato soup
2 T. oil
Salt and pepper to taste

1 med. green pepper, sliced
1 c. chopped celery
1 can cream of mushroom soup
2 c. milk
1 c. flour

(2 cans golden mushroom soup may be substituted for mushroom & tomato soup)

Salt & pepper venison steaks. Roll in flour and fry in oil just until brown. Saute' green pepper, onion and celery in butter until browned lightly. Place steaks and vegetables in baking dish. Add soups and milk; cover. Bake in 300 degree oven for 2 hours.

Yields 4 - 6 servings.

Roasts

Leg of Venison

1 - 6 to 8 lb. leg of venison
salt to taste
2 c. apple cider vinegar
4 bay leaves
dash of thyme
4 T. A-1 sauce

4 T. worcestershire sauce
4 T. soy sauce
1 cube of beef broth
1 tsp. minced garlic
8 bacon strips

Season venison with salt. Make small cuts into legs. Place in shallow pan. Combine all of remaining ingredients except beef broth and garlic. Pour over venison. Keep in refrigerator for at least 12 hours. Turn occasionally. Remove venison from marinade, reserving marinade. Place venison in baking pan. Lay the 8 bacon strips across venison and season with minced garlic. Bake at 450 degrees for 30 minutes. Reduce oven temperature to 325 degrees. Mix 1 cup of beef broth with 1 cup boiling water; pour over venison. Use remaining marinade to baste meat frequently. Bake at 325 degrees for 2 to 2 1/2 hours for medium rare or 3 1/2 hours for well done.

Yields 8 servings.

Slow-Cooker Venison Roast
with Vegetables

3 to 4 lb. venison roast
1/2 cup soy sauce
4 T. worcestershire sauce
seasoned meat tenderizer
1 T. garlic flakes

1 cube of beef bouillon broth
6 potatoes, quartered & pared
8 med. carrots, cut in 2" pieces
1 large onion, sliced
6 slices of bacon

Soak roast in vinegar water for 2 hours; rinse and dry. Cut wedges into roast. Sprinkle soy sauce and worcestershire sauce over roast; let stand for 1 hour. Add seasoned meat tenderizer and garlic flakes. Wrap roast in bacon slices and place in cooker. Add potatoes, carrots and sliced onions. Mix 1 cube of beef bouillon according to directions and pour into bottom of cooker. Cover and cook on slow heat for 6 1/2 hours or 3 to 3 1/2 hours on high heat.

Yields 6 to 8 servings.

Sweet and Sour Venison Pot Roast

3 1/2 lbs. venison pot roast
1 T. brown sugar
3 T. catsup
1 bay leaf
1 tsp. salt
3/4 c. water

2 T. fat
1 c. chopped onion
1/3 c. crushed pineapples
1/2 c. cold water
1 T. cornstarch

Melt fat in heavy kettle. Add roast and brown well on each side. Add onion, bay leaf, salt and 3/4 cup water. Cover and simmer 1 hour. Mix together brown sugar, vinegar, catsup and pineapples. Add to roast. Cover and continue to simmer about 1 hour or until roast is tender with touch of fork. Remove pot roast. Make gravy by skimming off excess fat from broth remaining in kettle, leaving only about 2 tablespoons fat. Combine 1/2 cup cold water with cornstarch. Mix until smooth. Gradually add to broth and stir until gravy is thickened. Serve gravy over roast.

Yields 6 to 8 servings.

Venison Roast and Noodles

3 to 3 1/2 lbs. venison pot roast
2 T. flour
2 tsp. beef bouillon granules
1/8 tsp. garlic powder
2 bay leaves
2 c. chopped onions

1/2 c. catsup
1/3 c. firmly packed brown sugar
1/4 c. lemon juice
1/2 c. crushed pineapple, drained
hot cooked noodles

Trim excess fat from meat and reserve. Cover meat with flour. In large sauce pan, heat trimmings to make 2 tablespoons of fat. Discard trimmings. Brown meat on both sides in hot fat. Add bouillon granules and 1 1/4 cups hot water. Spinkle with garlic powder. Add bay leaves. Sprinkle onions on top and around roast. Cover and bake in oven at 325 degrees for 1 1/2 hours. Remove bay leaves and discard. Mix together catsup, brown sugar and lemon juice. Pour over meat. Top roast with pineapples. Cover and continue to bake 30 to 40 minutes or until meat is tender. Serve with noodles.

Yields 8 to 10 servings.

Venison Onion and Mushroom Roast

1-3 lb. venison roast
1 pkg. Lipton onion soup mix
1 can cream of mushroom soup
salt and pepper to taste

Wash roast thoroughly. Salt and pepper and place in roaster. Mix soups together and pour over roast. Cover and cook at 400 degrees for 2 hours. Add water as needed to keep roast from drying.

Ethnic Dishes

Venison Burritos

1 1/2 lbs. ground venison
1 pkg. French's taco seasoning mix
1 can refried beans
1/2 pint sour cream
2 whole tomatoes, diced
1 cup onions, diced
2 cups shredded cheddar cheese
8 large flour tortilla shells

Brown venison in large skillet. Drain excess fat. Stir in taco seasoning mix & 1 cup water. Simmer 20 mins. Wrap tortilla shells tightly in foil. Heat in 400 degree oven for 20 mins. After heating, put into each shell, 2 Tbls. refried beans, 2 Tbls. venison. Top with cheese, onions, tomatoes and sour cream. Fold ends of shells in first & then fold each side over once. Serve with taco sauce if desired. Yields 8 servings.

Sweet & Sour Venison Steak

6 to 8 - 6oz. venison steaks
3/4 c. catsup
1/4 c. soy sauce
2 T. prepared mustard
1 clove garlic, minced or pressed
1/4 tsp. black pepper
1/2 c. dark corn syrup
2 T. apple cider vinegar

Soak steaks in 1 cup of vinegar & cover with water for 1 hour; rinse and dry. In small bowl, stir together catsup, corn syrup, soy sauce, vinegar, mustard, garlic & pepper until well blended. Place steaks in shallow roasting pan. Brush on sauce. Bake in 375 degree oven 1 to 1 1/2 hours or until tender, turning often and basting with sauce. Last 1/2 hour add remaining sauce and continue baking.

Teriyaki Venison Steak

8 - 6 to 8oz. venison steaks
1/2 c. soy sauce
2 T. brown sugar
1 clove garlic or 1 T. garlic flakes
1 small pce. gingeroot (optional)

Soak steaks for 1 hour in 1 cup vinegar and enough water to cover steaks. Rinse and dry. Mix all other ingedients in shallow dish; add steaks. Marinate for 1 hour. Cook steaks slowly until brown.

Yields 8 servings.

Chinese Venison with Rice

1 1/3 c. uncooked rice 1 T. salt
1/3 c. salad oil
1 1/2 T. soy sauce
3 c. boiling water
2 beef bouillon cubes
2 medium onions, chopped
4 stalks celery, chopped
2 green peppers, chopped
3 cups diced cooked venison

In large skillet, cook & stir rice in oil over med. heat until golden brown. Add salt, water, bouillon cubes & soy sauce. Cover tightly & simmer 20 mins. Add onion, celery, green pepper & venison. Cover tightly & simmer 10 minutes or until all liquid is absorbed & rice is tender.

Yields 4 to 6 servings.

Spanish Venison Steak

2 lbs. venison steak
1/2 c. flour
salt & pepper to taste
3 T. cooking oil
2 cans golden mushroom soup

1 c. catsup (opt. for tomato taste)
1/4 c. evaporated milk
1/2 c. sliced celery
1 medium onion, chopped
1/2 c. green pepper, chopped

Soak steak for 1/2 hour in vinegar water; rinse and dry. Roll steak in flour after seasoning with salt and pepper. Warm cooking oil in skillet. Add floured steaks. Fry on both sides until brown. Remove and place in baking dish. Mix all other ingredients and pour over steak. Cover tightly and bake in slow oven 300 degrees for about 1 1/2 hours or until tender.

Yields 5 to 6 servings.

Venison Lasagna (With Sour Cream)

1 - 8oz. pkg. lasagna noodles
1 1/2 lbs. ground venison
2 tsp. beef broth granules
1/2 tsp. salt
1/2 tsp. pepper
1/4 tsp. garlic powder
1 - 8oz. can tomato sauce

2 tsp. soy sauce
2 tsp. worcestershire sauce
1 T. brown sugar
1 c. cottage cheese
1 - 12oz. carton sour cream
6 green onions, chopped
1 c. grated cheddar cheese(mild)

Cook noodles to package directions; rinse and drain. Mix venison with soy sauce, worcestershire sauce and beef broth granules. Salt and pepper. Brown in skillet. Add garlic powder, tomato sauce and brown sugar. Mix well. Cook for 5 minutes. Remove from heat. Combine cottage cheese, sour cream and onions. Alternate layers of noodles, mixture and meat mixture in 2 quart baking dish. Top with cheddar cheese. Bake at 350 degrees for 35 minutes.

Venison and Vegetable Stir-Fry

1 lb. venison steak
3 carrots, sliced
1 qt. water & 1 c. vinegar mixture
1/2 tsp. sugar
2 T. red cooking wine
1 6oz. pkg. frozen pea pods, thawed
1/2 c. bamboo shoots
    (halved lengthwise)

1 1/2 c. broccoli-one inch pieces
1 tsp. salt
2 T. soy sauce
1 med. onion, cut in wedges
1/2 c. water chestnuts, sliced

Soak steak in vinegar/water solution for 2 hrs. Rinse. Place in freezer for 5 minutes. Remove & slice along grain into thin strips. Cook broccoli and carrots in boiling salt water for 2 minutes; drain. Mix cornstarch, salt & sugar; blend in soy sauce & cooking wine. Set aside. Preheat oil in wok on high heat. Stir-fry broccoli, carrots and onion in hot oil for 2 minutes or until tender. Remove from wok. If needed, add more oil. Add half of steak strips in hot wok and stir-fry 2 to 3 minutes or until brown. Remove; add remaining steaks and stir-fry 2 to 3 minutes. Add all meat, peapods, water chestnuts and bamboo shoots to wok. Stir in soy mixture. Cook and stir until thickened. Add broccoli, carrots and onion to wok. Cover and cook 1 minute more. Serve over brown rice.

Yields 4 to 6 servings.

Venison Peanutty Stir Fry

1 1/2 lbs. venison steaks, sliced into strips
2 tsp. beef bouillon granules or 2 cubes
2 T. cornstarch
1 med. onion, chopped
2 cans sliced water chestnuts

4 T. soy sauce
1 c. dry roasted peanuts
4 c. broccoli, chopped
2 T. cooking oil

Dissolve bouillon granules in boiling water; blend soy sauce and cornstarch together; mix with bouillon and set aside. Heat oil in wok on high heat. Stir-fry separately for one minute peanuts, onion & garlic, broccoli and water chestnuts. Stir-fry steak strips for 5 to 6 minutes. Add soy, bouillon mixture. Stir. Stir in vegetables and peanuts. Cover and cook 3 minutes. Serve over rice.

Yields 6 - 8 servings.

Burgers & More

French-Toasted Venison Sandwich

4 slices venison roast meat,
cut 1/4" thick
1 egg
2 T. milk
8 slices of bread

Put each slice of meat between 2 slices of bread. In medium-sized bowl, beat egg. Add milk to egg and stir. Dip each sandwich in egg-milk mixture and brown slowly on both sides in a little hot fat.

(For hot fat, use 2 T. of margarine to enhance flavor)

Yields 4 servings.

Venison and Cheese Loaf

1 1/2 lbs. ground venison
3/4 c. oats, uncooked
3/4 c. grated cheese of choice
1/3 c. chopped onion
1 tsp. salt
1/2 tsp. dry mustard
1 egg, beaten
3/4 c. milk

Preheat oven to 350 degrees.

Thoroughly combine all ingedients. Pack firmly into 8 1/2 x 4 1/2 x 2 1/2 loaf pan. Bake approximately 1 hour and 15 minutes. Let stand 5 to 10 minutes before slicing.

Yields 6 servings.

Venison Burgers in Barbecue Gravy

1 lb. ground venison
2 tsp. beef broth granules
1/2 c. cracker crumbs
1/4 c. dry bread crumbs
1/2 c. milk
1 egg
1/8 tsp. pepper
1 pkg. brown gravy mix
3 T. cooking oil
1/2 c. water
1/2 c. barbecue sauce
2 tsp. worcestershire sauce

Combine venison, bread crumbs, cracker crumbs, milk, egg, beef granules & pepper. Shape into patties. Roll in dry gravy mix; fry in oil in large skillet until brown. Remove from pan. Stir water, barbecue sauce & worcestershire sauce into drippings. Mix well. Return patties to skillet & simmer 10 minutes. Yields 4 to 6 servings.

Venison Stew

1/2 c. flour
1 tsp. salt
2 T. shortening
1 tsp. pepper
2 lbs. venison meat, cut into 1 inch pieces
6 c. hot water
1 bay leaf
3 pared med. potatoes, cut into 1 inch cubes
4 carrots, cut into 1" slices
1 green pepper, cut into strips
1 c. sliced celery
1/2 c. diced onion
1 T. salt
2 beef bouillon cubes

Mix flour, salt & pepper. Coat meat with flour mixture. In large skillet, brown meat in shortening. Add water. Heat to boiling. Reduce heat. Cover & simmer 2 hours. Add remaining ingredients. Simmer 30 more minutes or until vegetables are tender.

Venison Kabobs

2 lbs. venison steak, cut into
1 1/2 inch cubes
1/2 c. salad oil
1/2 c. catsup
4 T. & 1 tsp. vinegar
1 tsp. salt
1 tsp. pepper
1 to 2 cloves of garlic

Place venison cubes in bowl. Blend remaining ingreds. & pour over meat. Let stand in refrigerator about 4 hours. Place cubes on metal skewers. Broil 3" from heat in preheated broiler or on outdoor grill about 10 to 15 mins. Baste kabobs with marinade before serving. Cubes of tomatoes, mushrooms, green peppers or other vegetables may be added to skewer between meat cubes for meat & vegetable kabob.

Yields 6 servings.

Venison Meatloaf

1 lb. ground venison
1/2 lb. ground pork
1 1/2 c. finely chopped br. crumbs
2 eggs
1/4 c. chopped onion
1/2 c. green pepper (optional)
2 tsp. beef broth granules
1/8 tsp. celery salt
1/4 tsp. black pepper
2 tsp. worcestershire sauce

Mix thoroughly ground venison with 2 tsp. beef broth granules. Set aside. Mix chopped onion, green peppers, bread crumbs & eggs. Add ground pork; set aside. Mix celery salt, pepper & worcestershire sauce to venison mix. Now mix all ingredients together thoroughly; form into meatloaf pan. Bake at 350 degrees for 50 minutes to 1 hour.
Let stand 15 minutes before cutting.

Venison Meat Salad Sandwiches

1 c. ground cooked venison
1 T. chopped pickle, dill or
sweetened
1 1/2 T. chopped onion
3 T. salad dressing
1/2 tsp. salt
1/2 tsp. pepper
4 slices of bread
butter or margarine, softened

Mix cooked venison, pickle, onion &
salad dressing. Add salt & pepper.
Toast bread on one side. Spread
untoasted side with butter or
margarine & salad mixture. Place
sandwiches on broiler rack & broil
until meat mixture bubbles and
browns

Yields 4 servings.

Venison Skillet Supper

1 lb. ground venison
3/4 c. chopped onion
1/2 c. chopped green pepper
1 - 16oz. can sliced tomatoes
1 tsp. salt
1/2 tsp. black pepper
1 tsp. chili powder
1 - 6oz. can kidney beans,
washed and drained
2 c. corn chips

In large skillet, combine onion, green
pepper & ground venison. Cook over
medium heat until meat is brown.
Add tomatoes, salt, pepper and chili
powder. Stir. Cover & simmer on low
heat 10 minutes. Stir in beans until
well heated. Top with corn chips &
serve.

Yields 4 to 6 servings.

Venison Liver Gourmet

1 1/2 lbs. thinly sliced venison liver
4 T. flour
1 1/4 tsp. salt
black pepper
3 T. butter or margarine
3 T. cooking oil

2 cloves garlic, peeled
2 medium onions
1/2 lb. mushrooms
1 - 16oz. can tomatoes
(or 2 1/2 c. tomato juice)

Salt & pepper liver; roll in flour & brown on both sides in skillet with butter or margarine. In another skillet, mix oil, sliced garlic and sliced onions. Cook slowly until tender. Add cleaned, sliced mushrooms. Cover tightly and simmer 4 to 5 minutes. Sieve tomatoes and add to skillet. Continue to simmer. Pour sauce over browned liver. Cover and simmer 5 to 10 minutes according to doneness desired.

Venison Liver & Onions

1 1/2 lbs. venison liver
3 T. bacon fat
2 medium onions peeled and sliced
1 tsp. salt
black pepper, if desired

Heat bacon fat in skillet; add sliced onions. Sprinkle with 1/2 teaspoon salt. Cover and cook slowly until onions are tender, 5 to 10 minutes. Remove the onions into a hot dish and keep warm while pan frying the liver. Use the other 1/2 teaspoon of salt and sprinkle on liver along with black pepper and fry in skillet until done. Serve liver with onions on a hot platter. If making gravy with this, roll liver in flour and fry until brown. Then simmer in gravy with onions.

Venison Sloppy Joe's

1 lb. ground venison
1/2 c. chopped green peppers
1/2 c. chopped onions
1 tsp. salt
1/4 tsp. paprika
1 - 8oz. can tomato sauce

Brown in medium-sized frying pan, ground venison, green peppers and onions. Season with salt and paprika. Simmer 15 minutes. Add tomato sauce. Cover and simmer 30 minutes.

Yields 4 servings.

Venison and Onion Burgers

1 lb. ground venison
1 c. diced onions
4 T. worcestershire sauce
4 T. butter or margerine

In large bowl, thoroughly mix ground venison & diced onions. Separate & make 4 patties. In large frying pan melt margarine over medium heat; add worcestershire sauce. Place burgers in frying pan. Cover & cook until done, about 15 minutes, turning once. Serve on burger buns.

Yields 4 servings.

Venison Stuffed Bacon Rolls

1 lb. ground venison
12 slices bacon
1/2 c. chopped onion
2 cloves garlic, minced
1 egg
1/2 c. tomato sauce

3/4 c. bread crumbs
1 - 4oz. can sliced mushrooms, drained
2 T. parsley
1/4 tsp. salt
1/4 tsp. pepper

Partially cook bacon. Remove bacon from drippings and set aside. Cook onion and garlic in drippings until tender but not brown. In large bowl combine egg and tomato sauce. Stir in bread crumbs, mushrooms, onion mixture, parsley, salt and pepper. Add meat and mix well. Divide mixture into 4 parts. Form into meat loaf style rolls. Place 3 slices of bacon side by side on wax paper. Place meat at one end of bacon slices and roll up jelly-roll style. Secure with toothpicks if necessary. Place rolls seam side down in large baking dish. Bake in 350 degree oven for 45 minutes for medium well rolls.

Yields 4 servings.

Venison Stroganoff

1 lb. ground venison
1/2 c. chopped onion
1/3 c. butter or margarine
2 T. flour
1 tsp. salt
1 clove garlic, minced
1/2 tsp. pepper
1 - 4oz. can mushrooms, drained
1 can cream of chicken soup
1 cup sour cream
8oz. noodles

In large skillet, cook meat & onion in butter until meat is brown. Stir in flour, salt, garlic, pepper & mushrooms. Cook 5 minutes, stirring constantly. Reduce heat. Simmer uncovered 10 minutes. Stir in sour cream. Heat through. Serve over cooked noodles.

Venison Tomato Chili

1 lb. ground venison
2 tsp. beef broth granules
pepper to taste
2 tsp. chili powder or to taste
1 small green pepper
1 small onion
1 tsp. brown sugar
1 T. butter or margarine
1 - 16oz. can tomatoes
1 - 32oz. can tomato juice
2 -16oz. can red kidney beans
    or chili beans

Saute ground venison, beef broth granules, pepper, green peppers & onion in skillet. Drain. Add chili powder, juice & tomatoes. Cook on medium heat for 1 hour. Add butter, brown sugar & beans. Simmer for one hour. For more of a tomato taste, add 1/2 cup catsup.

Venison Stuffed Green Peppers

6 medium-sized green peppers
1 cup rice
1 lb. ground venison
1 tsp. soy sauce
2 tsp. beef bouillon granules
1/4 c. buttered fine bread crumbs

1 c.cooked tomatoes or tomato juice
1 small can beef broth
3 T. butter or margarine
2 1/2 T. chopped onion

Wash & core peppers. Saute' onion & celery in butter for 2 minutes. Cook rice until tender. Mix venison with beef bouillon granules and soy sauce. Add rice, bread crumbs and half of tomatoes to mixture. Add sauteed onion and celery mixture. Fill peppers with stuffing. Bake in a greased shallow pan at 350 degrees for 20 minutes. Then add beef broth and remainder of tomatoes and bake for 1/2 hour or until peppers are tender and meat is done. Serve immediately.

Yields 6 servings.

Venison Vegetable Pie

1 1/2 lbs. venison, 1" cubes
3 T. bacon fat
salt to taste
3 medium-sized potatoes
1 medium-sized onion

2 T. flour
1/4 c. cold water
2 - pie pastry crust for 9" pan
4 medium-sized carrots

Soak venison cubes for 1 hour in 1/2 cup vinegar and water to cover meat. Rinse and dry thoroughly. Brown lightly in bacon fat and cover with boiling water. Add salt and simmer covered for 30 minutes. Pare potatoes, wash and dice. Scrape and slice carrots and peel and slice onion. Add to meat with more boiling water if needed. Simmer until all are tender. Mix a flour and water paste and stir into simmering mixture to make a thickened gravy. Add salt and pepper to taste. Bring to a boil and pour into pie pastry. Cover with pie pastry and slice top for steam to escape. Bake in hot oven 425 degrees until both crust are done; approximately 1/2 hour.

Yields 5 to 6 servings.

Grilled Venison & Vegetables

1 lb. ground venison
1 sm. pkg. carrots
4 tsp. barbecue sauce
4 large aluminum foil strips
salt & pepper to taste
4 med. potatoes

Mix barbecue sauce in ground venison. Make 4 venison burger patties. Place one burger on each foil strip. Peel & cut carrots. Wash & slice potatoes, don't peel. Divide and place carrots and potatoes on foil with burgers. Salt and pepper vegetables. Wrap foil tightly around venison patties & vegetables. Cook on outdoor grill for 30 to 45 minutes.

Yields 4 servings.

Venison Mincemeat

16 qrts. raw venison
1/4 bushel of apples
4 qrts. cherries, pitted
4 T. allspice
8 tsp. cloves
10 c. apple cider vinegar
3 lg. boxes of raisins
14 c. sugar
8 tsp. cinnamon
8 c. cider
2 tsp. salt

Cook venison until done, grind meat. Divide meat into 2 cold pack canners. Divide apples, raisins & cherries & add to each canner. Mix together remaining ingredients & pour half of mixture into each canner. Cover & set over night in a cold place. Pack in freezer boxes & place in freezer.

Venison Goulash

1 lb. ground venison
2 tsp. beef bouillon granules
1 sm. onion, chopped
1 sm. green pepper, chopped
1/2 tsp. pepper   1/2 can corn
1/2 can mixed vegetables
1 can tomato soup
1 T. chili powder

Saute' ground venison, beef bouillon granules, onion, green pepper and pepper. Add vegetables and soup. Bring to a boil. Reduce heat; cover and simmer 10 minutes. Stir in chili powder.

Can be served over cooked noodles. Can be topped with shredded cheese or cheese slices.

Venison Steak Stew

4 thinly sliced venison steaks
1/2 c. flour
1/2 tsp. pepper
4 T. soy sauce
1/2 tsp. salt
1 sm. onion, chopped
1/2 c. veg. liquid
1 sm. can peas & carrots or mixed vegs.
8 med. potatoes, cubed
1 8oz. can tomatoe sauce

Marinate steaks in soy sauce for 30 minutes. Salt & pepper steaks; roll in flour. Brown in butter. Saute' onion in skillet. Remove steaks and onion & place in baking dish. Mix all remaining ingredients and pour over steaks. Cover and bake in 350 degree oven until potatoes and steak are tender. Serve with corn bread.

Yields 4 servings.

Venison Kidney Saute'

1 venison kidney
1 c. flour
1 medium onion, chopped
1 c. fresh mushrooms, sliced
1/4 teaspoon pepper
1/4 tablespoon soy sauce

1/2 c. vinegar
1/4 c. butter or margarine
1 medium green pepper, chopped
1 beef bouillon cube
1/2 T. worcestershire sauce
1/4 c. red cooking wine

Soak kidney in vinegar and 1 quart of water for 2 to 3 hours. Rinse, slice thinly. Salt and pepper and coat with flour. Saute' onions, green peppers and mushrooms in margarine. Remove from skillet and set aside. Brown kidney slices on high heat in pan drippings. Dissolve bouillon cube in 1 1/2 cups of boiling water; pour over kidney slices. Mix together remaining ingredients and pour over kidney slices. Cover. Reduce heat and simmer until meat is tender.

Yields 4 servings

SECTION TWO

OTHER WILD GAME RECIPES

TABLE OF CONTENTS

Suggestions for Marinating and Preparing Other Wild Game

Included in the following pages are recipes of duck, fish, pheasant, rabbit and squirrel.

For preparing duck, pheasant, rabbit and squirrel, it is best to soak overnight in water. This will help to thoroughly clean the game. It is very important to remove all shots from the wild game.

The best method for tenderizing is to scald this type of game. Also, cooking slowly on very low heat or quickly on very high heat, basting with butter or margarine, will help to achieve tender meat. Milk is a good method for tenderizing any type of wild game.

Some fish may have a strong flavor. Soaking in milk overnight or a couple of hours before preparing, will help to modify this strong flavor.

We suggest experimenting with our recipes by mixing recipes such as rabbit ingredients with squirrel or duck. This will help bring enjoyment and variety to the dinner table.

DUCK

John 3:16
For God so loved the world, that he gave his only begotten Son, that whosoever believeth in him should not perish, but have everlasting life.

Tasty Duck Fry

4 duck breast filets
1/2 c. flour
1/2 tsp. salt
1/4 tsp. pepper
1/4 tsp. nutmeg
1/4 tsp.paprika
2 eggs, beaten
2 T. oil

Wash duck filets. Mix together flour, salt, pepper, nutmeg and paprika. Roll each filet in flour and spice mixture. Fry in oil on low to med. heat for 1 hour or until tender and golden brown. Turn filets once.

Yields 4 servings

Duck Barbecue

6 Duck breast filets
Barbecue Sauce - See page -71-

Wash duck breast thoroughly. Place on hot grill for 10 minutes turning once. Brush with barbecue sauce and continue grilling for 20 minutes, brushing with barbecue sauce and turning often.

Yields 6 servings

Baked Cranberry-Orange Duck

6 duck breast   1 c. flour
1 can cranberry sauce   3 T. oil
1 can mandarin orange
salt & pepper to taste

Wash duck breast thoroughly. Sprinkle both sides of breast with salt & pepper. Roll in flour; fry in hot oil just until brown. Place breast in baking dish. Mix cranberry sauce and mandarin oranges together and pour over duck. Cover and bake at 300 degrees for 1 hour.

Yields 6 servings

Mushroom Duck

4 sm. duck
1 1/2 c. fresh mushrooms
1/2 c. butter or margarine
1 med. onion, chopped
1/2 c. flour
3 T. cooking wine
salt & pepper to taste

Wash duck thoroughly. In skillet, combine margarine, salt, pepper, cooking wine, mushrooms, onions, and flour. Cook on medium heat for 5 minutes. Stuff into each duck. Baste outside of duck with softened margarine. Salt and pepper. Bake at 450 degrees for 10 - 15 minutes.

Yields 4 servings

Holiday Duck Breast

6 c. of bread, toasted and broken
(wheat & white bread)
1 c. chopped apples
1/2 c. walnuts, chopped
1/2 c. raisins
1 stick butter, melted
1 tsp. salt
1/2 tsp. pepper

1/4 tsp. cinnamon
1/8 tsp. ginger
6 duck breasts
6 maraschino cherries
cinnamon
apple slices

Mix together bread, apples, walnuts, raisins, cinnamon, and ginger with 3/4 stick of melted butter. Brush duck breast with remainder of butter. Salt and pepper duck breast and place in baking dish cavity side up. Spoon in mixture on top of breasts; cover and bake for 1 hour or until breasts are tender. Remove to serving dish and add cinnamon, apple slices and maraschino cherries in center. Serve with lime jello salad for decorative dinner.

Stuffed Duck

4 small duck
salt and pepper to taste
1/2 c. green pepper, diced
1/2 c. celery, diced

1/2 c. onion, diced
1/4 tsp. sage
1/2 c. butter or margarine, softened

Thoroughly clean each duck. Rub insides with margarine, salt and pepper. Mix green pepper, celery, onion and sage. Stuff mixture into each duck. Rub the outside of each duck with softened margarine. Salt and pepper. Bake in preheated oven at 450 degrees for 10 to 15 minutes or until tender.

Yields 4 servings

Stuffed Goose

1 large goose
8 c. bread crumbs
1 c. onion, chopped
1 c. celery, chopped
1/2 c. butter or margarine
2 tsp. salt

1/4 tsp. pepper
1/2 tsp. poultry seasoning
1/2 tsp. sage
1/4 c. water
2 eggs, well beaten

Prepare goose by washing thoroughly. Baste inside of goose with softened margarine, salt and pepper. For stuffing, cook onion and celery in butter just until tender. Add to bread crumbs. Add seasonings and mix well. Add water and eggs. Stuff into goose. Baste the outside of goose with softened margarine. Sprinkle with salt and pepper. Wrap foil around legs. Bake uncovered at 325 degrees as follows:

Small goose	3-4 hours
Large goose	4-5 hours

FISH

Matthew 4:19
And he saith unto them, follow me, and I will make you fishers of men.

Delightful Halibut

1 lb. pkg. frozen Halibut filets
2 c. lettuce, chopped into small
pieces
2 green onions, chopped
1/2 c. slivered blanched almonds

2 cans mushroom soup
2 T. butter
1/2 c. diced celery
salt & pepper to taste

Salt and pepper filets to taste and arrange in baking dish; spread soup over fish. Saute' celery in butter and pour over fish. Bake at 400 degrees for 25 minutes. Before serving place lettuce on platter and arrange fish on lettuce; sprinkle fish with green onions and almonds. Add paprika for color and special taste.

Fresh Fish and Noodle Casserole

1 1/2 lbs. fresh fish
1 can cream of mushroom soup
1 - 4oz. can mushrooms
1 sm. onion, chopped
16oz. pkg. egg noodles

1/2 c. milk
2 c. mozzarella cheese, grated
2 T. margarine
salt and pepper to taste

Steam fish over boiling water for 20 minutes or until tender; salt and pepper. Boil noodles 6 - 8 minutes and drain. Mix all ingredients and place in a deep casserole dish.

Topping: 3 eggs
4 c. bread crumbs
1/4 c. margarine

Mix and top on casserole. Cover and bake at 350 degrees for 30 minutes.

Yields 6 to 8 servings.

Bluegills Delight

8 - 10 bluegills
1/2 c. corn meal
2 T. oil

1/2 c. flour
2 T. margarine
salt and pepper to taste

Mix corn meal and flour together. After thoroughly cleaning, salt and pepper both sides of fish; roll in corn meal, flour mixture. Heat skillet to 325 degrees with oil and margarine. Fry fish until golden brown, turning only once.

Cajun Style Bluegills

8 - 10 bluegills   extra spicy Mrs. Dash
1/2 c. corn meal   1/2 c. flour
2 T. oil   2 T. margarine

Mix flour and corn meal together. After thoroughly cleaning fish, sprinkle both sides liberally with extra spicy Mrs. Dash. Roll in corn meal and flour mixture. Heat skillet to 325 degrees with oil and margarine. Fry fish until golden brown, turning only once. Very tasty.

Tasty Fish Broil

1 T. chopped dill
1 T. lemon juice

1/2 c. melted margarine
4 lg. fish filets, cut into halves

Place filets in 13 x 9 cake pan. Mix lemon juice and melted margarine; pour over filets. Sprinkle each filet with chopped dill. Broil 10 - 15 minutes or until fish breaks apart with touch of fork. Serve with tartar sauce of choice.

Yields 4 servings

Fish Filet Bake

2 T. worcestershire sauce
2 T. soy sauce
1 T. lemon juice

1/4 c. melted margarine
4 lg. fish filets, cut into halves

Mix worcestershire sauce, soy sauce, lemon juice and melted margarine.
Marinate fish in marinade for 1 hour before baking. Bake in 350 degree oven
with marinade in uncovered baking dish for 30 minutes.

Yields 4 servings.

Best Ever Fried Fish

8 fish filets
1/2 c. flour
1/3 c. oil
1/2 c. corn meal
salt and pepper to taste

Mix flour and corn meal together. Salt & pepper both sides of filets. Heat oil in 325 degree skillet. Fry fish in hot oil until golden brown, turning only once. (Mouth watering; delicious with walleyes and small bass)

Yields 8 servings.

Fish Barbecue

8 lg. fish filets
1 lg. tomato, sliced
1 lg. green pepper, sliced
barbecue sauce of choice

Wash fish thoroughly. Place foil on grill. Add fish and grill until almost done. Brush each fish liberally with barbecue sauce. Add sliced green peppers and tomatoes. Cover with foil. Grill until fish flakes.

Yields 8 servings.

Lemon Baked Bass

2 T. margarine
2 T. lemon juice
1 lb. Bass
1 tsp. salt
1/4 tsp. pepper
1/2 tsp. marjoram
1/2 tsp. thyme
paprika
lemon wedges

Melt lemon juice and margarine in baking dish in oven; place fish in dish; coat both sides with lemon juice mixture; sprinkle onion and other ingredients over fish. Bake covered for 25 minutes; remove oven and sprinkle with additional paprika; serve with lemon wedges if desired.

White Fish Soy Bake

2 lbs. white fish
3 T. soy sauce
1 tsp. ginger
1/2 tsp. garlic powder
1 tsp. grated lemon peel
1/4 c. water
1/4 c. lemon juice
lemon slices
parsley

Place fish in ungreased 13 x 9 x 2 baking pan. Mix all ingredients except lemon slices and parsley. Pour over fish and cover. Let stand in refrigerator over night or approximately 8 hours. Drain mixture and reserve; broil fish 4 inches from heat, 6 minutes on each side. Brush on reserve mixture during baking time. Remove to serving dish. Add lemon slices and parsley.

Cod Fish Bake

1 lb. cod fish
1/2 tsp. salt (or to taste)
1/2 tsp. pepper
1/2 c. flour
5 T. margarine (or cooking oil)
2 T. dried green/red pepper flakes
1 c. fresh mushrooms, chopped
1 can cream of mushroom soup

Salt and pepper fish and roll in flour. Brown in skillet with margarine or cooking oil; remove and put in baking dish. Add to skillet dried green/red pepper flakes and fresh mushrooms; saute' for 8 to 10 minutes; pour over fish. Add mushroom soup and bake at 350 degrees for 20 minutes or until fish flakes easily. Serve over potatoes or rice.

Barbecued Salmon Strips

2 lb. salmon
1/4 c. oil
1 1/2 T. lemon juice
1 med. onion, chopped
2 T. butter
1 c. catsup
2 or 3 bay leaves
1/2 tsp. garlic salt
1/2 tsp. pepper

Place salmon strips in shallow dish. Combine oil and lemon juice. Pour over salmon strips. Chill for 45 minutes, turning every 15 minutes. In skillet saute' onion in butter until tender. Stir in catsup, bay leaves and seasonings. Place foil over grill and pour half of the sauce on foil; place fish on sauce; pour remaining sauce over fish. Cook 15 minutes on each side or until fish are tender. If using oven, place 1/2 of sauce in baking dish; place fish on sauce and pour remaining sauce over fish. Bake at 350 degrees for 30 minutes. Turn fish after 15 minutes.

Baked Cornbread Walleye

6 filet of walleye
salt to taste
1/2 tsp. pepper
1/2 c. flour

1 1/2 c. corn meal
2 eggs, beaten
1 T. lemon juice

Sprinkle lemon juice on fish and set aside for 5 minutes. Mix flour and corn meal mixture together. Salt and pepper fish, dip in egg batter, roll in flour and corn meal mixture and place in baking dish. Bake uncovered at 350 degrees until golden brown; turn and bake until other side is brown, approximately 30 - 40 minutes.

Flounder Filets

1 lb. flounder filets
salt and pepper to taste
1 c. sour cream

6 thin lemon slices
1 1/2 tsp. minced parsley
1 tsp. orange rind

Salt and pepper flounder filets on both sides and place in baking dish; top each piece of fish with sour cream and lemon slices. Sprinkle with orange rind and parsley. Bake at 350 degrees for 35 - 40 minutes.

PHEASANT

Romans 10:10
For with the heart man believeth unto righteousness; and with the mouth confession is made unto salvation.

Great Baked Pheasant
(Very Tender)

1 pheasant   1/2 c. flour
2 T. oil   2 c. milk
salt, pepper, nutmeg to taste

Clean pheasant thoroughly being sure to remove all shots. Leave legs and thighs attached. After cleaning, sprinkle both sides of each piece with salt, pepper and nutmeg; roll in flour and fry in oil just until brown. Place in baking dish; Cover with milk. Cover and bake in 300 degree oven for 2 hours.

Yields 4 servings.

Spiced Pheasant and Rice Bake

1 pheasant
2 c. water
2 c. rice
1/4 tsp. salt
2 T. margarine
1/4 tsp.pepper
Garlic salt and paprika to taste

Wash pheasant thoroughly; filet pheasant breast; leave legs and thighs attached. Place rice and water in deep baking dish. Add margarine, salt & pepper; stir. Sprinkle both sides of pheasant with garlic salt and paprika. Place on rice. Cover and bake 2 hours at 325 degrees.

Yields 4 servings.

Baked Pheasant

1 whole pheasant
1 bay leaf
3 celery leaves with some celery
4 slices bacon
1/2 c. bacon drippings
1 c. sliced mushrooms

1 lg. onion sliced
1 green pepper sliced
1/4 tsp. nutmeg
1/2 c. milk
salt to taste
parsley

Rub inside and outside of pheasant with salt and nutmeg. Place bay leaf, celery and celery leaves inside pheasant cavity. Place pheasant in baking dish. Fry bacon and pour bacon drippings over pheasant. Add mushrooms, onion and green pepper to baking dish. Pour milk over pheasant and bake at 350 degrees for 1 1/2 hours. Turn pheasant every 30 minutes basting with drippings in dish. remove bay leaf and celery leaves before serving and sprinkle with parsley.

Barbecued Pheasant

1 pheasant
Barbecue sauce:
1 c. catsup
1 c. coke
1/4 tsp. salt
1/4 tsp. paprika

1 clove garlic, finely chopped
1/8 tsp. turmeric
2 tsp. worcestershire sauce
1/4 c. onion, finely chopped
or 1 tsp. onion salt

Clean pheasant thoroughly. Filet breasts. Leave legs and thighs attached. For sauce, mix all ingredients in meduim saucepan; bring to a boil, boiling for 1 minute; cover and simmer for 30 minutes. Brush sauce on pheasant; prepare pheasant on grill, turning once and brushing with sauce often or place pheasant in baking dish; Cover with sauce. Cover and bake at 300 degrees for 2 hours.

Yields 4 servings.

Pheasant Fry

1 pheasant
1/2 c. flour
2 T. margarine or buttered flavor

2 eggs, beaten
garlic salt and pepper to taste
2 T. oil

Clean pheasant thoroughly. Filet breasts; keep legs and thighs attached. Dip each piece in egg then sprinkle both sides with garlic salt and pepper. Roll in flour. Place in 300 degree frying pan with oil and margarine or crisco. Fry until golden brown, turning only once.

Yields 4 servings.

Pheasant With Rice Stuffing

2 lb. pheasant
2 slices bacon
1 c. sliced mushrooms
2 stalks of green onion, finely
chopped
1 c. water
1/2 c. uncooked wild rice

1/4 tsp. nutmeg
2 T. slivered almonds
4 T. butter
1 tsp. lemon juice
1/2 tsp. salt
Salt and pepper to taste

Rub pheasant inside and outside with salt, pepper and nutmeg. Cook almonds, onions and rice in butter for 8 minutes, stirring frequently. Add water, chicken bouillon, lemon juice and salt. Bring to boil; reduce heat. Cover and cook for 20 minutes. Add mushrooms and cook for 5 minutes, making sure liquid is absorbed and rice is fluffy.

Lightly stuff pheasant with rice mixture. Place in shallow pan breast up. Lay bacon strips on pheasant. Cover and roast in oven at 375 degrees for 30 minutes. Then bake 1 1/2 hours uncovered. If bird seems dry brush with butter for remaining 15 minutes of cooking time.

Pheasant and Noodles

2 pheasants
1 - 16oz. pkg. of egg noodles
2 chicken bouillon cubes

3 T. cornstarch
mixed in 1/2 c. cold water
1 c. sour cream
salt and pepper to taste

Fill 5 quart pan with water. Bring to boil. Add bouillon cubes. Clean pheasants and thoroughly salt and pepper both sides of each pheasant; Add to boiling water and boil for 1 hour. Remove from heat. Bone pheasants, return to broth with noodles; boil approximately 10 minutes. Add sour cream and cornstarch and water mixture. Boil 2 minutes longer.

Yields 6 to 8 servings.

Pineapple-Pheasant Salad

2 whole pheasants
1 - 2 c. mozzarella cheese
1/2 c. slivered almonds
3 medium carrots
Salt and pepper to taste.

1 sm. to med. head lettuce
1 - 15oz. can chunk pineapple
2 sm. or 1 very lg. tomato
Ranch salad dressing

Clean pheasants thoroughly; sprinkle with salt and pepper. Place pheasants in crock pot with 1/2 cup of water. Cook on high for 4 hours or until pheasant begins to fall off of the bone. Wash lettuce and drain; wash tomatoes; peel carrots. Bone and cool pheasant. Chop drained chunk pineapple. Layer ingredients as follows: Lettuce, pheasant, carrots, cheese and almonds. Cut tomatoes into eight sections and place around salad on platter. Top with ranch dressing or top with dressing individually. Excellent main dish. Serves 6.

Pheasant Gelatin Mold

2 pkgs. lemon gelatin
1 c. cold water
1 c. mayonnaise
1 cooked and boned
pheasant, finely cut
1/2 c. seedless grapes

1 c. diced pineapples, drained
2 c. boiling water
3 T. lemon juice
1 tsp. salt
1/2 c. mandarin oranges, finely cut
1 c. celery, finely cut

Dissolve gelatin in boiling water; add cold water, lemon juice, mayonnaise and salt. Beat until well blended. Chill until partially set. Add remaining ingredients. Mold as desired and chill until firm.

Yields 8 servings.

Orange Sauce Mushroom Quail

3 quail
3 slices of bacon
Salt and pepper to taste
1/2 lb. fresh mushrooms (sliced)
1/2 bunch green onions (4 onions)
2 T. butter, melted

1 T. prepared mustard
1/4 tsp. dry ginger
1/2 c. orange marmalade
2 oranges, sliced
1/4 c. slivered almonds

Wrap quail in bacon; salt and pepper and place in baking dish. Saute' mushrooms and onions in butter and pour over quail. Bake for 45 to 60 minutes at 325 degrees making sure the quail is tender. Mix well the dry mustard, dry ginger and orange marmalade. Arrange orange slices on serving dish and place quail in center of dish. Spoon remaining ingedients over quail; sprinkle with slivered almonds and serve.

Roast Quail With Wild Rice

3 quail
1 c. wild rice
1 c. apple juice

1 apple, sliced
1/4 tsp. cinnamon
salt and pepper to taste.

Place quail on foil in baking dish. Salt and pepper quail. Cover quail with uncooked rice and apple juice. Wrap tightly with foil and bake for 50 minutes at 325 degrees. Open foil and place sliced apples over quail; Sprinkle cinnamon on apples; close foil and bake for 10 minutes and serve. Serves 4.

Saucy Quail

3 quail
1 med. onion
1 clove garlic; finely chopped
1/2 bay leaf
1/2 tsp. peppercorn
1 clove

1/2 c. butter
1/2 pt. white cooking wine
2 T. flour
1/2 tsp. salt
1/2 tsp. pepper
1/2 tsp. chives, finely cut

Combine onion, garlic, bay leaf, peppercorn and cloves in bowl and mix well. Saute' these ingredients in 1/2 of the butter for 6 minutes stirring constantly. Cut quail in half, place into sauce and add cooking wine. Simmer for 1/2 hour; remove quail and strain it; reserve sauce. Melt remaining butter in saucepan; blend in flour; stir in reserve sauce. Cook until thick and then add chives. Salt and pepper quail and place in baking dish; pour complete sauce over quail and bake for 15 minutes and serve. Serves 4.

RABBIT

James 1:12
Blessed is the man that endureth temptation; for when he is tried, he shall receive the crown of life, which the lord hath promised to them that love him.

Rabbit Dumplings

1 rabbit   1/2 tsp. salt
1/2 c. bacon drippings
1 egg beaten   1/4 c. milk
1 c. flour   2 T. oil
2 tsp. baking powder
1 tsp. Lowry's Seasoned Salt

Clean rabbit thoroughly. Soak overnight in water. Boil rabbit in bacon drippings and seasoning salt. Cook until tender. Bone rabbit and return to broth. Mix flour, baking powder and salt. Beat together egg, milk and oil. Add to flour mixture. Drop by tablespoonfuls into boiling broth. Cover and cook 15 - 20 minutes.

Yields 4 to 6 servings.

Rabbit Apple Bake

1 rabbit
1/4 tsp. curry powder
1 lg. can apple juice
3 - 4 apples   1/2 tsp. salt
2 T. butter   1/4 tsp. pepper
1/4 tsp. cinnamon

Clean and cut up rabbit. Soak in apple juice overnight. Drain rabbit. Reserve juice. Salt, pepper and sprinkle curry powder on rabbit and place in baking dish. Pour in 1 cup of apple juice. Bake for 1/2 hour. Peel and slice apples and place on top of rabbit. Slice butter on top of apples and sprinkle with cinnamon. Cover and bake for 1/2 hour or until rabbit is tender.

Southern Baked Rabbit

1 lg. rabbit   1 c. evap. milk
1 c. crushed cornflakes
or bread crumbs
1 tsp. salt   1/4 tsp. garlic salt
1/4 tsp. pepper
Softened margarine

Wash rabbit thoroughly. Cut in pieces. Soak in milk for 30 minutes at room temp. Mix cornflakes or bread crumbs, salt, pepper and garlic salt together. Roll rabbit in mixture. Dot each piece with butter. Bake in shallow baking pan at 350 degrees for over 1 hour, or until tender.

Roasted Rabbit

1 rabbit
1/2 c. chopped onion
1/2 c. chopped celery
3 strips bacon   1/4 tsp. salt
1/4 tsp. pepper
Softened butter or margarine

Clean rabbit thoroughly. Mix together celery, onion, salt and pepper. Stuff into rabbit. Rub rabbit with soft margarine. Place bacon slices over rabbit and secure with toothpicks. Bake at 350 degrees for 45 minutes.

Yields 4 servings.

Rabbit Fricassee

1 rabbit, cut in pieces
2 c. fresh mushrooms
2 T. cornstarch in 1/4 c. cold water
1 - 16oz. can tomatoes
2 T. cooking wine
salt & pepper to taste.

Wash rabbit thoroughly. Salt and pepper both sides of each piece; place in electric skillet. Mix together mushrooms, tomatoes and cooking wine. Pour over rabbit pieces. Heat in 300 degree elec. skillet. Add cornstarch. Simmer on low heat 1 1/2 hours or until rabbit is tender.

Yields 4 servings.

Baked Cottontail Rabbit

1 rabbit	1/2 tsp. nutmeg
1 med. onion	3 carrots, sliced
3 T. butter	1/2 to 1 c. flour

1 1/2 cans cream of chicken soup
1 stalk celery (cut 1/2" thick)
salt & pepper to taste

Clean and cut up rabbit; remove fat; boil for 1 hour. Remove. Salt and pepper to taste. Sprinkle nutmeg on rabbit and roll in flour. Brown rabbit in butter on med.high heat for 10 minutes. Place in baking dish. Place sliced onion, carrots and celery on rabbit and cover with soup. Cover and bake at 400 degrees for 1 hour or until rabbit is tender.

Vegetable Stuffed Rabbit

1 rabbit
4 carrots
2 celery stalks
1/4 tsp. pepper
2 strips bacon

4 med. potatoes
2 T. butter or margarine
1 tsp. salt
1/4 tsp. curry powder
2 c. water

Wash rabbit thoroughly. Peel and cook potatoes. Mash and add butter, salt, pepper, curry powder and celery. Stuff into rabbit; place rabbit with stuffed side down in baking dish. Peel carrots and place around rabbit. Place bacon on back of rabbit; secure with toothpicks. Pour 2 cups of water over rabbit. Cook at 400 degrees for 45 minutes or until tender. Just before done, remove bacon strips and allow rabbit to brown.

SQUIRREL

Psalms 112:1,3

... Blessed is the man that feareth the Lord, that delighteth greatly in his commandments. Wealth and riches shall be in his house; and his righteousness endureth forever.

Pineapple Squirrel Bake

1 squirrel, cut into pieces
1/2 c. flour
2 T. oil
1 can chunk pineapple
1/2 c. water   2 T. soy sauce
salt & pepper to taste.

Wash squirrel pieces thoroughly. Salt and pepper both sides of each piece. Roll in flour. Brown in oil in preheated skillet just until brown. Place squirrel pieces in baking dish. Mix together pineapple with juice, water and soy sauce. Pour over squirrel pieces. Bake at 350 degrees for 45 minutes.

Yields 4 servings.

Baked Squirrel With Orange Sauce

1 squirrel, cut in pieces

For sauce:
    1/2 c. orange marmalade
    2 T. spiced mustard
    1 1/2 T. brown sugar

Wash squirrel pieces thoroughly; place in baking dish. Make sauce and pour over squirrel pieces. Cover and bake in 350 degree oven for 45 minutes.

Yields 4 servings.

Squirrel Stew

1 squirrel
2 med. potatoes, cut into
small pieces
4 carrots, chopped
1/2 c. onion, chopped
2 T. cornstarch mixed in 1/4 c.
cold water
1/2 c. celery, chopped
1 chicken bouillon cube
salt & pepper to taste

Wash squirrel thoroughly. Place in 5 qrts. boiling water. Add bouillon cube, salt & pepper. Boil 30 minutes. Remove squirrel from broth and bone. Place squirrel back in broth. Add peeled carrots and potatoes, celery, onion and cornstarch. Cover and boil for 15 minutes; then simmer for 30 minutes longer or until vegetables are tender.

Yields 4 servings.

Sour Cream Baked Squirrel

1 squirrel, cut in pieces
1 tsp. salt   1/2 tsp. pepper
1/4 tsp. curry powder
1 med. onion, chopped
2 c. milk   1 1/2 c.sour cream
softened butter or margarine

Wash squirrel pieces thoroughly. Rub each piece, both sides with softened margarine. Mix together salt, pepper and curry powder. Sprinkle both sides of each piece with spice mixture. Place in baking dish. Mix together sour cream and milk. Pour over squirrel pieces. Cover and bake at 300 degrees for 2 hours.

Yields 4 servings.

Apple Baked Squirrel

1 squirrel   3 med. apples
1 tsp. cinnamon
2 T. brown sugar
1/4 c. margarine
1/4 tsp. nutmeg
salt & pepper to taste

Wash squirrel thoroughly. Peel and slice apples. Cut up margarine. Mix together, cinnamon, brown sugar and nutmeg; toss with margarine and apples. Stuff into squirrel. Place stuffed squirrel seam down in baking dish. Baste top of squirrel with softened margarine. Salt and pepper. Cover and bake at 300 degrees for 1 hour. Uncover and bake 30 minutes longer to brown. Yields 4 servings.

Mushroom Stuffed Squirrel

1 squirrel
2 c. whole fresh mushrooms
2 small cans mushroom gravy
1/4 c. butter or margarine
1/4 c. cooking wine
2 T. cornstarch mixed in 1/4 c. water

Wash squirrel thoroughly. Wash mushrooms. Boil mushrooms in margarine and cooking wine for 3 minutes. Add cornstarch. Boil 1 minute longer. Stuff into squirrel and place seam down in baking dish. Pour mushroom gravy over squirrel and bake at 300 degrees for 1 1/2 hours.

Yields 4 servings.

Basic Fried Squirrel

1 squirrel, cut into pieces
salt and pepper
1/2 c. flour
2 T. oil
2 T. margarine
2 c. boiling water

Wash squirrel thoroughly. Scald with boiling water. Salt and pepper both sides of each piece. Roll in flour. Fry in preheated oil and margarine on medium high heat for 40 minutes or until golden brown, turning only once.

Yields 4 servings.

Egg Battered Fried Squirrel

Follow instructions and ingredients for basic fried squirrel substituting garlic salt for regular salt and dipping squirrel in two beaten eggs before adding spices and rolling in flour. Very delicious.

Yields 4 servings.

Squirrel and Rice

1 squirrel, cut into pieces
salt, pepper, & paprika
2 c. rice   2 c. water
2 T. butter or margarine
parmesan cheese

Wash squirrel pieces thoroughly.
Sprinkle both sides of each piece
with salt, pepper and paprika. Place
rice, water and margarine in baking
dish. Add squirrel pieces. Sprinkle
each piece with parmesan cheese.
Cover and bake at 350 degrees for
1 hour.

Yields 4 servings.

Squirrel Salad

1 squirrel
1/2 c. mayonnaise
salt & pepper   2 slices bacon
1/4 c. finely chopped celery
1/4 c. finely chopped onion

Wash squirrel thoroughly. Fry bacon
crisp; crumble. Boil squirrel in
bacon drippings until meat is
tender. Cool and bone. Chop
squirrel into pieces. Mix squirrel
pieces, mayonnaise, bacon bits,
celery and onion. Add salt and
pepper to taste. Serve on lettuce or
rolls.

Yields 4 servings.

Squirrel Fricassee

Use basic rabbit fricassee recipe, page 83, adding 1/4 teaspoon of paprika for added flavor.

Squirrel Dumplings

Use basic rabbit dumpling recipe, page 81.

Vegetable Stuffed Squirrel

Use vegetable stuffed rabbit recipe, page 84

Baked Cranberry-Orange Duck recipe, page 52, May also be used with both rabbit and squirrel to add a tasty variety to the dinner table.

Genesis 10:8, 9
And Cush begat Nimrod: he began to be a mighty one in the earth.
He was a mighty hunter before the Lord: wherefore it is said, Even as Nimrod the mighty hunter before the Lord.
Isaac speaking to Esau his son:

Genesis 27:3, 4
Now therefore take, I pray thee, thy weapons, thy quiver and thy bow, and go out to the field, and take me some venison;
And make me savoury meat, such as I love, and bring it to me, that I may eat; that my soul may bless thee before I die.

A HUNTER'S PRAYER

Dear Heavenly Father
I thank you for the
beast in the field
that you permit me to eat.
I thank you for the
quiver and bow
The hands you give me
to prepare this savoury meat.
I pray now
that you'll be with me
as I go into
the woods and fields.
Give me wisdom
and lead each step I take.
Protect me from all harm
and keep safe those others all around
As each of us
mighty hunters we endeavor to become.

INDEX

INDEX (cont.)

INDEX (cont.)

Please send me _____ copy(ies) of Variety With Venison and Other Wild Game at the low price of $8.95 each, plus $1.25 postage and handling. For additional copies add .50 postage each. (Michigan residents please add 4% sales tax).

Name _____ Address _____

_____ Phone _____

Mail order with payment to:

Green & White Publishing Co.
2108 Spring Arbor Rd.
Jackson, MI 49203